What People Are Saying About

Hope and Witness in Dangerous Times

In these troubling times it's easy to feel "I'm too insignificant to make a difference." Brent Bill draws deeply on age-old and modern Quaker insights to show how each of us can find our own way forward from hopelessr⌐ and move through contemplation and onward into ac⌐⌐ ⌐gests that effective engagement in large and sma⌐⌐ ⌐e based on faith, prayer and love of othe⌐ ⌐f them!). And he firmly calls us t⌐ After all, if faith matters, it has to

John Lampen, autl. *and Branches*

Hope and Witness in Da⌐. ⌐s Times is at once simple, accessible and profound. It offers straightforward spiritual insights grounded in Quaker practice on how to live with integrity while seeking, in whatever way we are called, to help heal ourselves and the world around us.

Brent Bill has shown once more why so many of us turn to his writings to ground our spiritual journey. *Hope and Witness in Dangerous Times* is a tonic for the weary and a reminder of how we can live a life of wholeness in a chaotic time.

Barry Crossno, General Secretary, Friends General Conference

In this little book full of interesting insights and practical stories we learn how, in Quaker experience, hope and witness take root in the life of the Spirit. As individuals and society we all have unique experiences and blind spots, so we are exhorted not to judge and to back the efforts of others. With love as the prime motivation, Quaker worship and business method are anchors for finding God's direction for each of us, helping us to be

wholly integrated people.
Judith Baker, British Quaker Conciliator

Brent Bill's *Hope and Witness in Dangerous Times*, is an inspiring meld of Quaker history and day to day practices to deal with the challenges of today; a handbook, if you will, for facing the unknown with a surety and faith that truly transcends centuries. **Noel Paul Stookey**, singer/songwriter/activist, "Paul" of Peter, Paul & Mary

J. Brent Bill draws us into the depths of the Quaker spiritual imperative for action in the world, by providing very useful Quaker history and consideration for how our actions are rooted in the life of the spirit, in community, in worship, in prayer, and in love. He provides a reminder that even while we feel called to address injustice, we must examine our own blindness – our humanness – and it is by tending to the inner life that we embody God's spirit as the source of power. Brent challenges us to ask ourselves, "What is mine/ours to do?", discerning Jesus' example to be less critical and more invitational in how we live and act. Get ready to feel inspired! **Gretchen Castle**, General Secretary, Friends World Committee for Consultation – World Office (Quakers)

Hope and Witness in Dangerous Times is very simple but powerful at the same time, just as love and faith are. This book reminds us of the integrality that Christianity and any spirituality must have. It will be a real light in the lives of many people and situations. **Miguel Costop**, Director, PROGRESA: The Guatemala Friends Scholarship Program

Hope and Witness in Dangerous Times

Lessons from the Quakers on Blending Faith, Daily Life, and Activism

Hope and Witness in Dangerous Times

Lessons from the Quakers on Blending
Faith, Daily Life, and Activism

J. Brent Bill

CHRISTIAN ALTERNATIVE
BOOKS

Winchester, UK
Washington, USA

JOHN HUNT PUBLISHING

First published by Christian Alternative Books, 2021
Christian Alternative Books is an imprint of John Hunt Publishing Ltd.,
No. 3 East St., Alresford, Hampshire SO24 9EE, UK
office@jhpbooks.com
www.johnhuntpublishing.com
www.christian-alternative.com

For distributor details and how to order please visit the 'Ordering' section on our website.

Text copyright: J. Brent Bill 2020

ISBN: 978 1 78904 619 9
978 1 78904 620 5 (ebook)
Library of Congress Control Number: 2020942258

A CIP catalogue record for this book is available from the British Library.

Permissions
"Citizen of Dark Times" used by permission of Red Hen Press and Kim Stafford, from Wild Honey, Tough Salt. Copyright © 2019 by Kim Stafford.
Tiny Pricks Projects guidelines used by permission of Diana Weymar.
Lyrics from "It's Impossible Until It's Not" and "Lean into the Light" used by permission of Carrie Newcomer.

Design: Stuart Davies

Printed and bound by CPI Group (UK) Ltd, Croydon, CR0 4YY
Printed in North America by CPI GPS partners

We operate a distinctive and ethical publishing philosophy in all areas of our business, from our global network of authors to production and worldwide distribution.

Contents

Also by J. Brent Bill

Beauty, Truth, Life, and Love: Finding an Abundant, Good Life with God

Holy Silence: The Gift of Quaker Spirituality

Life Lessons from a Bad Quaker: A Humble Stumble Toward Simplicity and Grace,

Finding God in the Verbs: Crafting a New Language of Prayer (with Jenny Isbell)

Awaken Your Senses (with Beth Booram)

Sacred Compass: The Way of Spiritual Discernment

Mind the Light: Learning to See with Spiritual Eyes

Imagination and Spirit: A Contemporary Quaker Reader

Acknowledgements

I am grateful for the many friends and Friends who supported the development of this book.

First among them is Jennifer Kavanagh. A wonderful writer and Quaker, Jennifer first suggested that I take part in the "Quaker Quicks" series at a gathering of Quaker writers, editors and publishers in South Carolina, USA a few years ago. I appreciated her thinking I could make a contribution to the series but didn't pursue it immediately. Over the ensuing years in our correspondence, Jennifer kept bringing the subject up. I'm glad she did.

Other Friends who encouraged this work, though they may not realize it, are the Quakers of College Park Quarterly Meeting in northern California. They invited me to spend a day with them in January 2019 looking together at the topic of "Prophetic Witness and Hope in Difficult Times." Preparation for that day, and our time together, were the seeds from which this book sprang.

Finally, two Friends made editorial and other contributions to this effort. The first is John Lampen who is a British Quaker activist and the author of a number of fine works on Quaker hope and witness. The second is my dear, long-time friend Donna Higgins Smith of northern California, also an activist, who read many drafts of this manuscript and offered helpful critique, suggestions, and support.

Bless you all – and your good work in this world.

Citizen of Dark Times
by Kim Stafford

Agenda in a time of fear: Be not afraid.
When things go wrong, do right.
Set out by the half-light of the seeker.
For the well-lit problem begins to heal.
Learn tropism toward the difficult.
We have not arrived to explain, but to sing.
Young idealism ripens into an ethical life.
Prune back regret to let faith grow.
When you hit rock bottom, dig farther down.
Grief is the seed of singing, shame the seed of song.
Keep seeing what you are not saying.
Plunder your reticence.
Songbird guards a twig, its only weapon a song.

Introduction

Another school shooting. Children dead or dying or in the hospital or heading home physically safe but traumatized by what they've been through. With the air still filled with the smell of cordite and smoke, the airwaves and internet feeds immediately fill with people reacting. Some say things like "These children and their families are in our prayers." Others demand an immediate change in gun control laws. Those crying for legislation often deride those who say they're praying – "Praying doesn't accomplish anything" – and maintain that prayers are empty, hollow gestures. Those public people who say they're praying then mock the gun control activists as knee-jerk reactionaries who don't really care about kids and are merely using this tragedy to push their long-held agenda.

In the face of such a tragedy and this hostile back and forth, what's a person of faith to do?

Do we pray?

Do we act?

Quakers say it's not either/or but rather that it's both/and.

Certainly, prayers are needed and are more than hollow gestures. Prayer takes us, our hearts, and our concerns into the presence of our loving God who is grieving this horror with us. Prayer changes things because, for one, it changes us. It opens our hearts in love to those who have been wounded physically, emotionally, and spiritually. Prayer is something we can do in community, to offer grace and sympathy to the hurting children and suffering parents. Prayers which come from heart and soul, rather than merely being political pronouncements from pontificating posers, are felt as love by the sorrowing. We've witnessed that time and again at candlelight vigils, memorial gatherings, and more.

Prayers are important also because they can help us. As

1

we pour out our hearts, we hear our own concerns about this instance and others like it clearly. Perhaps in new ways. Prayers can clarify what our response should be; how we should act. And action is needed. As James says, "Faith without works is dead."[1] Charles Schulz the creator of the American comic strip "Peanuts" put it a bit differently and more graphically. He said the same thing slant when he portrayed Linus and Charlie Brown bundled up and walking through a snowstorm. They see Snoopy shivering in the snow. "Snoopy looks kind of cold, doesn't he?" observes Charlie Brown. "I'll say he does," responds Linus. "Maybe we'd better go over, and comfort him." So the boys come close to the shivering Snoopy. Linus looks down and says, "Be of good cheer, Snoopy." "Yes, be of good cheer..." echoes Charlie Brown. Then they walk away, leaving Snoopy shivering, with a big question mark over his head.[2]

Yes, action is needed. But action that is not rooted in a deep spiritual life can be dangerous and hollow – at least for Christians and other people of faith. That's because then it can too easily lapse into my political views and feelings, which are "always right," versus your political views and feelings, which are "always wrong" when they don't agree with mine. It becomes easy to demonize and vilify and move away from being the friends of Jesus we're invited to be. We lapse into partisan rhetoric which makes us easy to dismiss by those whose views are different from ours. "Oh, he's just saying that because he's a XXX" or "Of course, she feels that way. All XXXs do."

Unmoored from a life in the Spirit, we become ineffective at a time when effectiveness is called for. We appear shrill and uncaring, when we want our voices to be heard precisely because we care so much.

Combining personal faith with spiritual activism in the world has been a hallmark of Quaker faith and practice for going on four hundred years. The Religious Society of Friends, as Quakers are formally known, have been working for peace, equality, integrity, care for the earth, and more, not out of do-goodism, but out of be-goodism. Their work around the globe for women's rights, abolition of slavery, civil rights, immigration reform, public education, gender equality, peace, has always grown out of a deep understanding that Christian faith must be wed to daily living and addressing the needs of the human family, especially the downtrodden and oppressed.

Friends take seriously the example of Jesus who preached and healed. Who ministered and fed the hungry. Who taught his disciples and crossed accepted cultural boundaries to reach out to the despised. Who said to his followers:

> "For I was hungry and you gave me something to eat, I was thirsty and you gave me something to drink, I was a stranger and you invited me in, I needed clothes and you clothed me, I was sick and you looked after me, I was in prison and you came to visit me."
>
> Then the righteous will answer him, "Lord, when did we see you hungry and feed you, or thirsty and give you something to drink? When did we see you a stranger and invite you in, or needing clothes and clothe you? When did we see you sick or in prison and go to visit you?"
>
> The King will reply, "Truly I tell you, whatever you did for one of the least of these brothers and sisters of mine, you did for me."[3]

Quakers took the name Friends from the fifteenth chapter of John where Jesus tells his followers, "You are my friends if you do what I command. I no longer call you servants, because a servant does not know his master's business. Instead, I have called you friends, for everything that I learned from my Father I have made known to you."[4] To be the Friends of Jesus. What a glorious invitation. But it's an invitation that includes – "if you do what I command." And Jesus, by his example and teaching, demonstrates that what he learned from his Father is that faith is neither solely personal devotion and prayer or outward justice activism. It is a unified life of personal spiritual deepening and action that grows out of that deepening.

All of us are invited into such a holistic life. As the early Quaker William Penn said, "True godliness doesn't turn us out of the world, but enables us to live better in it, and excites our endeavors to mend it... Christians should keep the helm and guide the vessel to its port; not meanly steal out at the stern of the world and leave those that are in it without a pilot to be driven by the fury of evil times upon the rock or sand of ruin."[5]

I invite you to consider how your personal faith life better enables you to live in these dangerous times and how it moves you to work at mending the world. How do your spiritual beliefs empower you to help guide the vessel of the world and its people in a good and safe direction?

Throughout the coming pages we'll look at how Quakers have endeavored to live such lives (and don't always get it right!) and what lessons they might have for us. We will examine what motivated them, how they've acted and continued to act, and how we decide what we're called to do, what our spiritual work in this world is to be. For some of us it might be the grounding work of contemplation and prayer that supports the efforts of those on the front lines of the Lamb's War. For others it might be to become, in the words of the Quaker civil rights activist Bayard Rustin, "angelic troublemakers."[6] For many of us, it may well be some combination that may not have occurred to us up until now.

Regardless, we'll explore how our faith is not just about the hereafter, but it's also about here.

After all, if faith matters, it has to matter now!

Chapter One

Quakers, God, and Society: Where It All Began

"After all, if faith matters, it has to matter now!" That's how I ended the introduction. I did so because we are living in dangerous times. We're witnessing the growth of authoritarian leadership and social control, increasing partisan, racial, and religious violence at many levels, the erosion of accepted ways of thinking and interacting civilly, huge economic disparities, and more.

Ours are not the only times that have been dangerous. In Jesus' time and the beginning of Christianity, they were certainly dangerous. Look at what happened to Jesus and many of his earlier followers. Likewise, in the mid-seventeenth century, when Quakers began, they were dangerous. Perhaps that's one reason why, for a faith tradition known as being peacemakers, Quakers have long been a contrary lot. Quirky. Cranky. At least when it comes to political power, social injustice and the like. It's in our religion's DNA. Let's look at why that is.

Quakers, you see, were born in the maelstrom of the English Civil War. This was a time of great unrest in England – politically, socially, religiously. Politically there was the Puritan revolution and the establishment of the Commonwealth. As monarchists fought against the Puritans, huge armies surged back and forth across England, each seeking to win the population and nation to their side.

Socially it was the beginning of a shift from a more agrarian society to an industrial one. Urban areas were developing or redeveloping. Do any of these changes remind you of shifts in society today?

Religiously, Anglicans, Puritans, Catholics, and Dissenters/

Independents all were out proclaiming their ways of faith and worship. Unlike the American Civil War, which certainly had its religious component, but claimed to be (depending upon whether you were from the north or south) about saving the union and ending slavery or states' rights and economic dependency on slavery, the English Civil War had religion as a central issue. Since England had a state church, the various factions pushed their positions and hoped, by gaining the government, to impose their style of religion – and all it entailed – upon the English public at large.

Many of the groups of the time, not surprisingly, blended politics and religion. The Fifth Monarchy Men, for example, were political zealots who wanted to institute the biblical fifth monarchy of Daniel 2:44 ("And in the days of these kings shall the God of heaven set up a kingdom, which shall never be destroyed: and the kingdom shall not be left to other people, but it shall break in pieces and consume all these kingdoms, and it shall stand forever."[1]). Mostly Baptists, they were opposed to representative government and wanted to establish the reign of Christ and his saints.

Another group was the Muggletonians, named for Lodowick Muggleton, a London tailor. Muggleton was a Hellfire and damnation Puritan to the extreme. He believed the only true ministers had hair shorn short. He often had "revelations" – one of which was that his group was to seal the "elect and reprobate with eternal seals of life"[2] and then Jesus would visibly appear in power.

It's obvious from the above that the Civil War radicalized many people. Englishmen were recruited into militias on both sides. The late Quaker writer and wag John Punshon once remarked to me it was as if England had been overrun with Jehovah's Witnesses with guns!

Some of those recruited to the militias were men who helped form the early Quaker movement. George Fox, considered by many to be the founder of Quakerism, while in prison for his subversive preaching, was offered a reduced prison sentence if he'd serve in a militia. He refused. And so did many others who became Quakers. In doing so, they formed the basis for the first Quaker social action stand – what today is known as the Peace Testimony.

While Quaker faith may seem relatively tame today, in the years of the English Civil War and immediately following, it was radical. And considered extremely dangerous and subversive.

The Quakers (formally known as the Religious Society of Friends) grew out of a movement known as the Seekers. The Seekers came into being in the early seventeenth century and drew from various religious groups including independents, Puritans, Anglicans, and even some Catholics. They used a silent form of worship feeling that the only constructive religious posture was to wait for divine initiative. They rejected all outward sacraments, paid ministry, and church order. That's because they felt that religious life should consist of deep spiritual experiences and such things could not be state ordered, ordained, or dependent on which Christian faction controlled the government.

George Fox, born in 1624 in Drayton-in-the-Clay, was deep in a life filled with his personal spiritual unrest as a young man. His village was a Puritan stronghold. His weaver father, prominent in the area, was known as Righteous Christer. Fox agreed with Puritans that, because of sin, the gulf between divine and human was something the human could not cross without divine intervention. Still the forms and practices of the Puritans left him spiritually unfulfilled and seeking. Looking for spiritual solace, he visited those he called the "priests" (Puritan ministers) and "professors" (professing Christians) for advice – which varied from "smoke tobacco" to "get married."

Finding this advice unhelpful at best, Fox despaired. He withdrew from religious company. Then, "When... I had nothing outwardly to help me, nor could tell what to do, then, oh then, I heard a voice which said 'There is one, even Christ Jesus, that can speak to thy condition.'"[3] When he heard, he records, his heart leapt for joy.

So fortified, he began sharing his message that Christ Jesus could speak in and to every person's spiritual needs. The Seekers warmed to Fox's words of the immediacy of Christ's presence. Fox also spoke to them of his "openings" (revelations) – one of the main ones being about Light.

His message was that the Light of which he preached was that of God within, which he also described as "your Teacher," "your Guide," "the Anchor," and "the Inward Christ." He was not referring to intellect or conscience, but rather the working of God in our souls. His Light is the "true light that lightens every man who comes into the world."[4] This encounter with the Light as early Friends' experienced was not always pleasant and soothing. Many times it pointed out their sin or failings. Still, the inward Light is the basis for the Quaker admonition that we should look for that of God in each person. This principle, which continues to this day, is the basis for much of Quaker hope and witness throughout the generations.

From the Seekers, Fox began to gather the group that became known as "Quakers" in 1647. They were committed to reviving primitive Christianity – which they felt had been lost. Their understanding was that Primitive Christianity eschewed creeds, priests, rites, rituals, church buildings, tithes, hierarchy, a state church, and other norms of English religious and civil life in the day. They believed (and Quakers still do) that the Divine could speak directly to the individual and lead them aright spiritually. They traveled widely throughout England and the world spreading this message and speaking their truth. In fact, one of the early names for themselves was the "Publishers of Truth." As Geoffrey Durham says:

From their beginnings in the mid-seventeenth century, Quakers have made it their business to expose the anomalies they regard as injustices and do all they can to put an end to them. They have regularly found themselves in opposition to the spirit of the age as it fails to notice the evils lurking "in the system of things."[5]

This did not endear them to the religious authorities in England – Puritan, Anglican, Catholic, or otherwise. Persecution – because of the instability of the times – and paranoia ran deep. Of course, it could be argued that you are not paranoid if they are indeed after you, which at times for all English governments in this period, they were. The Fifth Monarchy Men, for example, attacked the government in 1661, in anticipation of Christ's return in 1666 (a commonly held belief of the time). Many, including those who became Quakers, believed that they were living in the last days of humankind.

To quench the perceived danger of all this civil and religious unrest, a spate of laws was passed to suppress dissenting religions. These edicts affected the early Quakers in no small part due to their unconventional worship, odd speech and views on class equality, willingness to confront civil authority, and theology. A few of these laws include:

- The Act of Uniformity (1662) – tried to establish "comprehensive church," integrating Puritans, Anglicans, et al. It failed but denied Quakers (and other dissenter faiths) their civil rights for over two hundred years.
- Treason Act (1661) – was aimed at Fifth Monarchy Men but ended up being used to send 4000 Quakers to prison.
- Quaker Act (1662) – one of the few aimed directly at the Quakers. It required oaths and disallowed meetings of five or more at a time. Conviction of third offense was punishable by "transportation" to the colonies.[6] William

Penn, one of the best known of the early Quakers, was tried under this Act. His case became famous because the jury refused to convict him. This incensed the judge who wanted Penn found guilty and he threw the jury in jail for defying his wishes.

There were more but this will give you an idea of the tenor of the times. Quakers, refusing to be part of or supportive of the state church, going so far as to disrupt their services with arguments and refutations of their theology, often found themselves in trouble. And in those days finding oneself in trouble often meant finding oneself imprisoned. At times there were as many Quakers in prison as out, it seems from the records they kept.

Because of their radical views they often found themselves lumped with those who were a violent threat to the government, such as the Fifth Monarchy Men. Their response brings me to a thread that runs throughout this book – that Quaker social witness is rooted in its understanding of faith.

The first Quaker public statement that is well known today is "A Declaration from the harmless and innocent people of God, called Quakers" to King Charles II in 1660. In it the Quakers state, "all bloody principles and practices, we, as to our own particulars, do utterly deny, with all outward wars and strife and fightings with outward weapons, for any end or under any pretence whatsoever. And this is our testimony to the whole world."[7] And then the Quakers go on at length citing the Bible and their spiritual beliefs to support their position.

Now, in all Quaker honesty (since integrity is one of the Quaker testimonies), I must say that this statement was not just a statement against war and fighting. No, it was written in no small part to put distance between the Quakers and the notorious Fifth Monarchy Men. The early Friends wanted the king and parliament to stop persecuting them out of fear that the Quakers might mount an anti-government army like the Fifth

Monarchy Men and march on London. Hence the "harmless and innocent" phrase in the title.

It is a form that the best of Quaker activism has followed to this day. That social action – whether against Trident submarines being based in Britain or immigrant families being separated along the United States' southern border – is rooted in more than a vague do-goodism. It is a tree that springs from a deeply planted spiritual seed and bears fruit. It is something that can be clearly stated in the religious principles that fertilize it.

And, like a tree it continues to grow and change throughout its seasons. If it is to provide shade and fruit, that is.

Today's Quaker peace testimony has evolved from the original declaration to Charles II. It still contains many of the same elements, but is much broader than George Fox, Richard Hubberthorn, Francis Howgill, and the other signers imagined. It is no longer just about a particular nation's civil and religious situation. Rather, it is about daily personal peace-making conduct and non-violence in all facets of life – personal and national and international. The peace testimony has changed to fit the times as the times changed.

In the same way that the peace testimony first arose out of Quakers' personal stake in proving the government needn't throw them in prison out of fear of an armed revolt, one could make the case that Quakers' interest in prison ministry first sprang from the fact that so many of them were in prison themselves and experienced the horrible conditions of those hellholes. They first ministered to their own. But early on they became involved in prison reform and criminal justice issues. In seventeenth-century Pennsylvania, William Penn abolished the death penalty for all crimes except pre-meditated murder. He also introduced the idea of productive labor for those incarcerated.

When Elizabeth Fry, born of parents prominent in two English banking families and who married into a third, first visited London's Newgate Prison over one hundred years after

Penn's reforms, she found the women there living in conditions that had not changed significantly since the seventeenth century. In 1816 she funded a prison school for the children who were imprisoned with their mothers. In 1817 Fry helped found the *Association for the Reformation of the Female Prisoners in Newgate.*

Such reform efforts have continued, including today's Alternatives to Violence Project (AVP). This organization began at New York's Green Haven Prison in the mid-1970s as a way to teach prisoners non-violent conflict resolution. This grassroots, primarily volunteer-led program, has been embraced by prison authorities and inmates around the globe as one that makes a positive difference in prisoners' lives.

Historically, Quakers are often known for their work for the abolition of slavery. What is often not known is this work began mere decades after Quakerism began. In 1688, in Germantown, Pennsylvania, four Quakers (Francis Daniel Pastorius, Garret Hendericks, Derick op den Graeff, and Abraham op den Graeff) drafted the first religious statement against African slavery. Now known as the Germantown Quaker Petition Against Slavery, it condemned slavery – including that practiced by (hold your breath) Quaker slaveholders. It argued that every human has basic rights regardless of their color or other circumstance. Though some historical records indicate the Quakers took it seriously, by a variety of circumstances the petition was "lost" for almost 150 years.

The seed had been planted though and various individuals including Benjamin Lay and John Woolman in the United States and Samuel Hoare Jr. and William Dillwyn in Britain worked to abolish the slave-trade and slaveholding. In 1776, Philadelphia Yearly Meeting banned slaveholding among Quakers.

The Germantown Petition was found 1844 and was used in the growing abolition movement in the US, which often involved Quakers, including their work on the Underground Railroad. After slavery was abolished in Britain and the United States,

Quakers continued to work for equality of all, including notably in the US, the work of Bayard Rustin in the twentieth-century's United States' civil rights movement.

Quaker work against slavery continues to this day, particularly regarding human trafficking. This is in no small part because, as Tim Gee writes:

> Racial inequality... can manifest throughout society, including in movements for peace. This need not lead to paralysis so much as to the exact opposite; there are points of intervention every day where oppression and capacity for violence is being built which can instead be transformed into moments to progress towards peace. It also means acting with movements for racial justice as vigorously as working against wars.[8]

While this work, based as it was in spiritual principles, was laudable and important and ahead of its time in many ways, it is also important to note that it was carried out imperfectly by imperfect people. Many early Friends, as Quakers are today, were people of their time. As such, they possessed some of the social views and biases of their contemporaries. Hence while many Quakers were for freedom for enslaved people, not all of them were willing to associate or worship with people of color. Today's Quakers are ashamed of and repent of such attitudes. Still, those earlier Quakers' attitudes remind us that being ashamed is not enough – instead, we need to seek out the seeds of similar kinds of biases in our own lives and, with Divine assistance, eliminate them.

The above examples show how Quaker work and witness – and hope for creating a beloved community of God on earth – began and evolved as society and its issues evolved. Such evolution has been a pattern for Quaker hope and witness throughout the years. And through the years, Quakers have learned a few things that can guide all of us who want to live lives that blend faith, our daily life, and activism.

The above examples also illustrate how faith has to matter now. No matter when that "now" is.

Chapter Two

Lessons Learned

Quakers have long had a reputation as being on the right side of history on things such as slavery, women's rights, gender equality, and more. But as I mentioned previously, while we may have been ahead of the social and religious curves on these things, we haven't always gotten it exactly right. For example, as I mentioned earlier, there were Quaker slaveholders in our early years. Even after Quakers disavowed slaveholding and advocated for the abolition of slavery, many white Friends did not welcome people of color into their meetings. Or if they did, they had in place segregated seating areas keeping the races apart. If you'd like to learn about these particular Friendly failings, read *Fit for Freedom; Not for Friendship: Quakers, African Americans, and the Myth of Racial Justice* by Donna McDaniel and Vanessa Julye.

Likewise, Quakers are well regarded for our fair dealings with native peoples. Again, while Friends in earlier generations often had more advanced views and actions than did their co-religionists in such interactions, they were at least partially blinded by the societal norms of their day. One glaring example is the nineteenth-century operation of Indian Boarding Schools by Quakers. As one teacher at the Quaker Tunesassa Indian Boarding School in New York, wrote, "We are satisfied it is best to take the children when small, and then if kept several years, they would scarcely, I think, return to the indolent and untidy ways of their people."[1]

Friend Paula Palmer felt led to start the "Toward Right Relationship with Native Peoples" project. She has researched the ways Native children were ripped from their families, given non-native names, and more by well-meaning Quakers. As

Palmer writes, "The multigenerational trauma of the boarding school experience is an open wound in Native communities today." She and others are leading the effort to educate Quakers and others about this long-ignored past. She also works with Quakers to heal the wounds of the past and labor for "a positive present and future for Native peoples."[2]

I could enumerate other times we've fallen short of our ideals, but by now you've got the idea. Despite our failings, Quakers have learned a number of important things over the years – lessons that can guide us, and others, in our witness and work in dangerous times.

- We have our blind spots.

In this way we are like the Quakers who preceded us. Some of these shortcomings are ours by virtue of living in the times we do. We can be too often blinded by societal norms and attitudes. That is not an excuse for our actions and attitudes, any more than it was for those Quakers who went before us. As Eva Pinthus said, "The duty of the Society of Friends is to be the voice of the oppressed but [also] to be conscious that we ourselves are part of that oppression. Uncomfortably we stand with one foot in the kingdom of this world and with the other in the Eternal Kingdom."[3]

So, even while we are doing good, we must keep in mind that we are not perfect. We need to take the time to examine how our attitudes are influenced by our positions in society. We would also do well to remember that future generations will have insights and societal norms that will make ours seem lacking. That being the case, we must undertake our work with humility and a constant reexamination of our motives, ideals, and understandings.

- Spiritually based activism is rarely confined to one topic.

John Woolman, for example, who is best known for his efforts to eradicate slavery, was also concerned about Native American issues of his time, care of the earth, and peace work. Elizabeth Fry, whose work with the women of Newgate Prison I previously mentioned, was also concerned for the homeless and pleaded for the abolition of slavery. Spiritual and social justice issues are often intertwined. In fact, they almost always are. The effects of slavery and racial hatred impact socioeconomics and education and even care of the earth. Advocating for peace means that we need to live simple lives and be careful that the things we buy do not mean harm for others, through poor wages or destroying the land they live on, or even as a cause for conflict or war. Our hope and witness are integrated testimonies to our faith and how we practice it. As Harvey Gillman wrote:

> The word 'testimony' is used by Quakers to describe a witness to the living truth within the human heart as it is acted out in everyday life. It is not a form of words, but a mode of life based on the realisation that there is that of God in everybody, that all human beings are equal, that all life is interconnected. It is affirmative but may lead to action that runs counter to certain practices currently accepted in society at large. Hence a pro-peace stance may become an anti-war protest, and a witness to the sacredness of human life may lead to protests against capital punishment.[4]

- Our hope and witness must be rooted in the life of the Spirit.

In the same ways Woolman, Fry, and the Quakers before and after them did, we must feed our souls at the same time we are feeding the physically hungry. We must cultivate peace in our inner lives if we wish to have an effective peace witness in the world. We must try to be integrated people – spiritually, emotionally, mentally, and physically. We dare not neglect spiritual nurture and practice. This is not easy but is necessary. It is far too easy to either be consumed by action and the work that must be done or to retreat into an interior contemplative life and stay there. To quote Eva Pinthus again:

> Seldom can we keep the inward and outward working of love in balance, let alone the consciousness of living both in time and in eternity, in timelessness. Let us not be beguiled into thinking that political action is all that is asked of us, nor that our personal relationship with God excuses us from actively confronting the evil in this world. The political and social struggles must be waged, but a person is more and needs more than politics, else we are in danger of gaining the whole world but losing our souls.[5]

- Worship is an amazing anchor for spiritual activism.

Rufus Jones, D. Robert Yarnall, and George A. Walton proved that in the twentieth century when they visited Nazi Germany shortly after Kristallnacht. The three Americans sailed under no illusion that great changes could be achieved, including their hope of extensive migration of Jews from Germany and relief for those in direst circumstances (including being held in concentration camps). Their proposed actions had been planned in consultation with Jewish leaders and other relief organizations. Still they continued, out of faithfulness to their call. Said Jones, "We shall do our best and wisest and we shall go in the strength of God."[6] Though they tried to keep their visit quiet, word leaked out and quickly reached Germany. The Nazi minister of propaganda, Joseph Goebbels, wrote a newspaper article mocking the Quakers as "the three wise men."

After various efforts, they were finally granted permission to meet with officers of the Gestapo. These men had the power, if they so chose, to allow the Quakers' relief efforts to proceed. However, upon the Quakers' arrival and presentation of their papers, the officers withdrew to meet with Gestapo chief Reinhard Heydrich. Instead of fretting or pacing, Jones, Yarnell, and Walton decided to have a period of Quaker worship right there. Jones reports it was a time of "deep, quiet meditation and prayer." After almost half an hour, the officers came back and reported the Quakers' requests had been granted. Sadly, as we now know, WWII broke out the next autumn, curtailing most of the planned relief work.

A more modern example of the power of worship in the face of a spiritual social concern has been demonstrated by the Earth Quaker Action Team (EQAT). EQAT was founded in late 2009 by Quakers from Philadelphia Yearly Meeting. In 2010, it launched its first action, asking PNC Bank, which has some historic Quaker roots, to withdraw financing from corporations engaging in mountaintop removal coal mining that causes huge and long-lasting environmental damage. For five years, EQAT members took part in non-violent direct action against PNC. This included having Quaker worship in various PNC branches and in shareholders' meetings. In March 2015, PNC changed their policy of investing in this destructive mining practice.

The examples of "three wise men" and EQAT show that though Quaker worship is rooted in silence, it does not mean that we are to keep silent in our witness. No. Our being rooted in silent worship is for listening for that which is beyond us and within us – that which is Eternal, as the early Quakers used to say. When we do so, we arise empowered with a holy boldness. We are spiritually centered and can speak out against injustice and for that which is right. That holiness and centeredness is oft times recognized by others, who respond to it.

- We must work in and from community, not alone.

Rhiannon Grant reminds Quakers that:

> We are not... a 'Do It Yourself' religion, but a 'Do It Ourselves' religion. Although no *special* person or object is needed to access divine wisdom, Quakers also admit the possibility that any individual might be mistaken – perhaps led astray by their personal desires. It's the group, not just the individual, which seeks to find the will of God.[7]

Participation in a spiritual community is especially important if we want to keep our work and witness centered in more than our own thoughts and ideas. While Friends in my neck of the Quaker woods often jokingly paraphrase Jesus' words to say, "Where two or three Quakers are gathered, there are four or five opinions," we really do rely on corporate discernment and support.

That's because time and the Spirit have taught us that there's a collective spiritual wisdom in a community of faith. If we are prepared to listen to it, that is. Quakers have often practiced spiritual discernment via a process known as a clearness committee. A clearness committee is a group of Quakers who gather to help a Friend determine a way forward with a leading they're wrestling with – from a new job to a marriage to... well, most anything. And that includes engaging in work and witness. As we practice collective discernment of the Spirit's leadings, "we are all being tested together," according to the contemporary Quaker Marion McNaughton.[8] As Craig Barnett notes:

> The community supports and challenges individuals to examine the origins of their leadings, to test whether they originate from the Spirit or from unacknowledged personal motives. At the same time, individual leadings challenge the whole community to reflect on its faithfulness to the promptings of the Spirit, and how it is being called to respond

to this new insight.[9]

When the meeting gathers in support, we go forth buoyed by that support and surrounded by love and light. Such support is especially needed when the work feels ineffective or we get discouraged.

• Spiritual activism must go beyond partisanship.

It is easy to get involved when a particular person whose policies, attitudes, and actions offend us comes into office. We get heated up and work against that person. But when power is restored to the correct side (according to us), we fade away. We lose interest. That's because for many of us it's hard to sustain work based on anger and hate and partisanship.

This is true in the era of Donald Trump in the US. Many progressives, including people of faith, were incensed by his immigration policies – rightfully so. But many of those same people of faith were quiet when some of the same things were occurring during President Obama's administration. We liked Barack Obama and so gave him a pass.

True hope and faithful witness have to be consistent across party lines no matter who is in power. Such work is easier to maintain if our hope and witness are rooted in that which is deeper than indignation, abhorrence, or hatred of a particular person in power.

Activism that results in deep change must be more than a political movement. Otherwise it easily loses steam. That is obvious in the United States when we look back at the number of young adults, particularly men, who were attracted to the Quakers due to our peace testimony. Many of us (but not all – we are an imperfect people), stood against the Vietnam war. While a number of young people stayed with Friends, like my friend the writer Scott Russell Sanders who first encountered peace loving Quakers in Oxford during that time, a number dropped away after the fear of them being drafted evaporated. This paralleled the decline of the anti-war movement in the US. The mass protests quickly faded as the threat to white middle-class Americans vanished. The work for the "revolution" as it was often proclaimed during the mid to late '60s faded away for many because it had been rooted in fear and loathing instead of a lasting commitment to true social revolution against all war, all racism, all poverty, and so forth.

One hundred years ago, Lucy F. Morland called us to remember that:

'Politics' cannot be relegated to some outer place, but must be recognised as one side of life, which is as much the concern of religious people and of a religious body as any other part of life. Nay, more than this, the ordering of the life of man in a community, so that he may have the chance of a full development, is and always has been one of the main concerns of Quakerism.[10]

• Spiritual activism must have love as its prime motivation.

At its best and most effective, our work must spring first from love.

I mentioned John Woolman and his concern for Native Americans earlier. In his journal, he writes that:

Having for many years felt love in my heart towards the natives of this land who dwell far back in the wilderness, whose ancestors were formerly the owners and possessors of the land where we dwell, and who for a small consideration assigned their inheritance to us, and being at Philadelphia in the 8th month, 1761, on a visit to some Friends who had slaves, I fell in company with some of those natives who lived on the east branch of the river Susquehanna, at an Indian town called Wehaloosing, two hundred miles from Philadelphia.[11]

In 1763 he set out to meet with Native Americans in western Pennsylvania in the midst of what was then known as an Indian uprising. As he pondered why he felt called by God to go he records that:

> Love was the first motion, and thence a concern arose to spend some time with the Indians, that I might feel and understand their life and the spirit they live in, if haply I might receive some instruction from them, or they might be in any degree helped forward by my following the leadings of truth among them.[12]

"Love was the first motion." What a remarkable notion! What a challenge to our action – does it first come from love?

The most important lesson of all. Quakers, at their best, have learned that when spiritual social witness is connected with love – of our fellow humans, the earth – then it is rightly guided and more effective than when love is absent. That doesn't mean we are any less rabble-rousers. It does mean that, regardless of what others think, we are acting out of what the apostle Paul claimed was the more excellent way – the way of Love.

When we pull all these lessons together, Quakers have found that our hope and witness are more effective. That's because they are not only improving or remedying human situations, but that they then speak to that of God in the people we work with and for. We point beyond our own human efforts to the great revolutionary kin-dom of God – the family of life and love.

As Roger Wilson said:

> As Christians we need to see ourselves as God's plumbers, working on tanks and channels for the living water that can

quicken the daily life of men, women and children... Jesus taught us about patterns of living that make for wholeness as we and our neighbours care for one another and build one another up. And all the patterns that Jesus showed us of cisterns and channels of caring and service challenge the patterns of Mammon that offer quicker and more showy results, but that end in the debris of a possessive society that allows the living water to run away into the sand. Good plumbers build to last; they don't fall for fashions that rust and fade and crack.

Seventeenth-century Friends were good plumbers. In and out of season, in and out of jail, in and out of court, counting house and farmstead, our Quaker forebears challenged the conventions of the day – in politics, in commerce, in the law, in the established church, in social etiquette, in education, in attitudes to war, poverty and crime. In face of the sterile institutions of their day they found living answer about the ways in which men and women might go about their business of living together.[13]

Though in this chapter I have primarily written about nurturing our own souls, Quakers have learned that doing work that is rooted in our spiritual life also nurtures the souls of those we work for and with. That is not to say we do this work in order to proselytize or convert others to the Quaker way. We don't. Not that our small faith group wouldn't welcome new members! Indeed, we would.

But we do this work not to convert individuals to our faith but rather to convert the structures and systems that hold people in bondage or keep them from being full human and fully spiritual – whatever that means for them. When we do this well, it is a healing gift we give to our fellow children of God.

We do speak our spiritual truths – sometimes in words. Sometimes in preaching. But ultimately, our work is rooted not in conversion of individual souls but rather being faithful to the call that the Divine has laid on our hearts and souls. When we do that, then we can hopefully point the way to what Roger Wilson called the living water that quickens their daily external and interior lives.

May we continue to do so with hope and faithful witness.

Amen.

Chapter Three

Doing Good While Being Good

One of the dangers of doing good is trying to do good in our own power. When we do that, we forget the reality is that our witness and activism reflect the actual values of our interior lives. Which may not be the same values as those we proclaim to hold.

Thus, if we want to be faithful activists we must tend to our spiritual lives. That way we can be certain that our activism does not devolve into something that is based solely on anger (righteous or not), partisan politics, or fueled by hatred toward those whose policies and actions we find abhorrent.

Grounding our hope and witness in our interior lives also reminds us that, no matter what we are told, real power does not reside in Washington, D.C., or London, or Moscow or any other world capital Rather, real power resides in that which is beyond political machinations and partisan connivings. Real power has always been rooted in spiritual power. Martin Luther King, Jr. knew that. He grounded his work in the life of the spirit and in the belief that "Evil may so shape events that Caesar will occupy a palace and Christ a cross, but that same Christ will rise up and split history into A.D. and B.C., so that even the life of Caesar must be dated by his name. Yes, 'the arc of the moral universe is long, but it bends toward justice.'"[1]

Remembering this guiding principal of King and others opens us to tending our spirits.

In the same way that Quakers follow George Fox in believing that Christ is our inner teacher, we also believe that we can learn much from studying Jesus' life on earth. His earthly life was one, according to the gospels, of taking time out of service to refresh and renew, to pray and meditate. In that way, he modeled his own words that the wise person builds on rock, not sand. Built on rock, it can withstand the storms and floods. Built on sand, it will be washed out and fall with a great crash.

A century ago, William Charles Braithwaite said:

> Seeking to live at all times in a divine order of life, Quakers have always counted social service part of Christianity. In fidelity to the genius of their inward experience, they have set themselves the task of developing their own spiritual sensitiveness to the light of truth; and have then resolutely confronted the unawakened conscience of the world with the demands of the new light, and have borne witness to it with undaunted patience.[2]

That may a bit lofty – especially the undaunted patience part – but Quakers have worked throughout the generations for the betterment of the human condition and earth on which we live. This work has been powered by our attempts to live in line with our understandings of the gospel of Jesus and the leadings of our Inner Teacher. The movement of the spirit inwardly has resulted in outward action, often in concert with other people, in the great social causes of various ages. When we work with others, we can bring a bit of spiritual leaven to what otherwise looks like a secular or partisan undertaking. In the past and present, we've endeavored to rid the world of those ills which harm the least of these as Jesus called them in the parable I referred to earlier – the homeless, the defenseless, the hungry, the widows and orphans, and more. Whether they are literally or metaphorically homeless, hungry, et al.

The Light of Christ illuminates our spirits so that we not only see the darkness in our lives but so that we can also behold it in the world. With a clear spiritual vision, we can then work with God in redeeming this world. The contemplative life leads us close to the heart of our loving God. It creates the desire to be the hands and feet and heart of that great love in this world.

The truth is our activism and attitude will model whether our inner and outer lives are in sync. If we are to work for peace, for example, our inner lives must be study halls for learning the way of personal peace. Jo Vellacott writes, "The people whom I know who live a truly nonviolent life are in touch with the source of power, call it what you will; the Light, the seed, God, the holy spirit."[3]

Being in touch with source of power can be achieved in a number of ways – corporate worship, individual meditation, spiritual reading, prayer. We need to find spiritual practices that nurture our interior lives and energize us to continue our activism – whether it be on the frontlines of demonstration or writing letters and calling legislators or spending time lifting those on the frontlines when we ourselves cannot do that work.

Prayer is one of the practices for me. I find prayer – deep prayer – especially helpful. As Gordon Matthews says:

If our spirituality can reach the depths of authentic prayer, our lives will become an authentic witness for justice, peace and the integrity of creation, a witness which becomes the context for our prayer. Out of the depths of authentic prayer comes a longing for peace and a passion for justice. And our response to violence and injustice is to pray more deeply, because only God can show us the way out of the mess that the world is in. And only God gives us the strength to follow that Way.[4]

Prayer reminds me to look for that of God in others – including the others whose actions and policies I stand against. It does so if I pray for them, taking time to hold them in God's Light and Love and asking that the Divine direct them in new ways (which may not, gasp, be my way!).

When I pray for such people, I am reminded that while I am often very certain of the correctness of my position, I see in part, not in whole. I see what I see from my own limited understanding. In praying for another, especially one who is in opposition to my position, I am inviting God's spirit to humble me. Such a prayer helps me to test my own views in light of what I know of the Divine will.

This sort of compassionate, searching prayer also reminds me that rarely am I convinced of a new way of thinking or seeing or to change my behavior by someone who obviously despises me and doesn't have my best interests at heart. I can accept correction and education from people who care for me – even if their words are hard to hear and sting. Centuries ago, William Penn said, "They have a Right to censure, that have a Heart to help: The rest is Cruelty, not Justice."[5] Prayer invites me to ask if I truly have a heart to help. Or if I just want to be right. Or just want to win the cause. Even at the cost of my own spiritual health.

Such prayer is hard work. But it is necessary work. It is exceedingly difficult to lift someone to God when you hate them. Or feel as if you do. My most effective prayers are ones where I pray for the wisdom and courage to see those others as fully human. To understand their pain or trouble or sorrow. To feel how they love those close to them and their hearth and home. To wonder how we might talk about the things dearest to our hearts over a glass of wine or a meal.

Jesus commands us to love our enemies and to pray for them that hate us. That's when some variation of the S.O.B. ("son of a bitch") prayer, as my friend (and Friend) Connie taught me, comes in helpful. "God, give that S.O.B. everything I would hope for myself to be made happy, whole, and free."

Part of the reason for praying that prayer is that it helps me to remember to look for that of God in others – even the political S.O.B.s. And it also helps me remember that they may consider me a S.O.B.

Another reason I pray is that prayer reminds me that love is, as the apostle Paul says, the more excellent way. And so I pray for the strength to be open to love, to love in the same way I am loved by my family, and my friends, and God. To say in prayer, on God's behalf and my own, *I love you, I love you, I love you.* Until I come to mean that love in my spirit and show it in my actions as a result of my encounter with the Great Lover of my Soul that has softened my heart and my pride, even while strengthening my resolve to work for justice.

The key, Connie says, to the S.O.B. prayer is that, "You don't have to mean it but you have to say it at least once a day for at least two weeks, every time you think of the jerk! It'll change you."

Which is one thing I need to remember. I need changing, too. I am not the perfect person with all the answers that I often think I am. When I'm honest with myself, I know that I'm snarky, self-righteous, always ready with the "right answer," and intolerant of others whose positions on everything from politics to religion are different than mine. I need humbling. I need to be humble. Japanese Quaker and diplomat Inazo Nitobe's prayer helps me move to the deeper, better spiritual place that my soul wants to dwell in:

I ask for daily bread, but not for wealth, lest I forget the poor.
I ask for strength, but not for power, lest I despise the meek.
I ask for wisdom, but not for learning, lest I scorn the simple.
I ask for a clean name, but not for fame, lest I condemn the lowly.
I ask for peace of mind, but not for idle hours, lest I fail to hearken to the call of duty.[6]

Taking time for our inner lives also helps us avoid what Thomas Merton called, referencing some words of Quaker Douglas Steere, the "pervasive form of contemporary violence to which the idealist most easily succumbs: activism and overwork."[7]

The call to duty is all around us. The needs are many. We want to rush out and do something. Prayer keeps us from rushing and helps us discern what small part of the huge number of tasks around us we are personally or corporately called to do. If we don't take this time for spiritual reflection, our doing, doing, doing does violence to our souls – and the work. Instead of ending conflict, we create more simply by creating it within ourselves as we find ourselves pulled in this direction or that. Action or family time? Social justice or prayer? The push and pull can become too much. Though we are busy doing good, it isn't as effective as it could be because we have not tended the roots that caused it to spring forth. We have not watered the plant. It withers and dies.

Tending the inner life is an exercise in human wholeness. It focuses our spirit in the same way action can focus our minds and physical selves. To be truly faithful to our hope and witness, we need both body and soul, mind and spirit, inner and outer.

As we are in touch with that which is Eternal, we are better able to do the work to which we are called. That's because it engages us in being fully human.

Also, as we nurture our interior lives, it helps us be rightly ordered, to see our true place in this universe. Too often, when I am caught up in doing good, I can place myself at the center of the universe. It too easily becomes about me – my solutions, my actions, my wisdom. I forget I am but one of the over seven and one half billion children of God sharing this planet. Every one of whom is loved by the Divine as much as I am.

When I am centered in my spiritual life, then I realize that I am not called to do this in my strength or out of my own will. Rather, I am being invited to do as I would unto God, as Jesus said in Matthew 25:45. In that, my work, while large for me, is but a part of the work being done on God's behalf and at God's beckoning in the world. I can then say, with Brother Lawrence, "accept the work that I do: I do it unto Thee."[8]

And in so doing, rooted in Spirit, I do it out of the great Love for and from God, even while being an "angelic troublemaker."

Chapter Four

Being For

"I don't want to be an anti, against anybody. I simply want to be the builder of a great affirmation: the affirmation of God, who loves us and who wants to save us."[1] So said the martyr priest Oscar Romero. Romero, though he was not a Quaker, expresses Friends' hope and witness when it's at its best. Especially in a time when so much activism is framed as what people are against. We are against this president or prime minister. We are against this policy or that action.

I'm not denying that there are things that are in opposition to deep faith and the gospel. They are legion. But in the Quaker tradition, true spiritual activism and spirituality are rooted, at their best, in positivity. We are for social justice. We are for clean water and good food for all people. We are for healthcare. We are for peace. Saying what we are for is an invitation to life and hope rooted in God's goodness. It is life calling to life.

Rufus Jones, writing about Yarnall, Walton, and his trip that ended with them holding worship in Gestapo headquarters, said:

We have come to Germany at this present time to see whether there might be any service which American Quakers could render, and to use every opportunity open to us to understand the present situation. Those whom we are to consult should clearly understand that we have had close and friendly relations with the German people throughout the whole post war period. We represent no governments, no international organizations, no parties, no sects, and we have no interest in propaganda in any form.[2]

The three wise men spoke of how Quakers had come to Germany in 1919 and helped feed, at times, over a million children a day and brought cows and coal – all without asking what side the people receiving aid were on.

Now were Jones, Yarnell, and Walton supporters of the Nazi regime? No, of course not. To be sure they opposed its policies and actions as the evil they were. But, to gain access to the highest levels of power where a change could possibly be wrought, they framed their mission in light of what they were for. These Quakers were for people as having the Light of God within and serving that light. This is a winsome way of speaking to others, including, or even especially, to those we are bringing a witness to. This way calls them to the Light within themselves. If, that is, we truly believe the Quaker principle we say we espouse.

This is in many ways more difficult than standing in opposition. It's easy for me to say what I'm against, especially when my dander is up. I am against mean policies that harm people. I am against the lotteries that entice people to squander money in an attempt to get rich quickly. I am against... on and on and on. But I've found reframing my positions or beliefs in a way that I am able to say what I am *for* is an exercise in spiritual development. For one, it challenges my thinking and helps me put it in the light of my interior life. This reframing also humbles me, which is something I often need. It gives me a sense of spiritual clarity; a clear vision of what is mine to do and say – and how to say it. After all, we may be called to speak truth to power – but what good is doing so if we cannot be heard because of the way we're saying it?

Now, I have some Quaker friends who disagree with me about this. They fear I'm advocating niceness or civility for their own sakes and to avoid conflict. I'm not. Conflict is around us. We need to engage it. And too many of us, Quakers included, engage in the sin of niceness to avoid conflict – what I call pacifist-aggressive behavior. I want to state firmly that I'm not opposed to loving confrontation and honest talk. But I am remembering how we are called to look for that of God in others. As people who want to be the friends of Jesus, we do well to follow his example.

Being for isn't about being "nice." It's about being true to seeing that of God in others while standing for things consistent with my understanding of the gospel of Christ my Inward Teacher. Some activists feel it is fine to vilify those they oppose. I admit that I don't comprehend how a spiritual activist can do that and remain grounded. As Quakers, who say we are the friends of Jesus, we do well to remember that Christ reserved his criticism for the religious people of his time. They were the ones who were certain that they had the truth and then sided with empire to protect their position. The people of empire themselves, however, Jesus won over by love and respect. One only has to think of the story of the chief tax collector Zacchaeus in Luke 19. Jesus invites himself to Zacchaeus' home for a meal. He treats Zacchaeus as a person of worth. Through this act of hospitality, Zacchaeus' life changes – he moves from the Roman Empire to the Kingdom of God.

In another example, Jesus invites Matthew to become one of his disciples. Like Zacchaeus, Matthew was a tax collector. Or to put it in today's terms, a staff member in much hated administration. Jesus' invitation incensed some religious leaders and activists. They criticized him for eating with tax collectors and sinners. To which Jesus answered, "I came not to call the righteous, but sinners to repentance."[3]

If you read the accounts of Jesus' encounters with Matthew and Zacchaeus, you don't see any record of Jesus getting into their faces and vilifying them. He wins them by sharing meals; talking to them with the respect one child of God should show to any other child of God. The respect a person of faith should show to any other – especially a person whose faith calls them to look for that of God in the other.

Looking for that of God in others isn't easy. Well, it's easy to say. But it's harder to do, especially when there is conflict between us and the other. But as Diana Lampen wrote:

If we mean it, we have to live it. That is why some of us in Northern Ireland do speak to the men of violence. It does not mean we agree with what they do. It does mean believing in the good that is in everyone and in the potential for growth and change that is in us all.

Some of our closest friends used to be involved in violence and have changed. I have learnt so much from them and their courage in changing, and I am encouraged to believe that anyone can change.[4]

Jones, Yarnell, and Walton went into the heart of Nazi darkness in this spirit. The organization that Jones, Yarnell, and Walton represented was the American Friends Service Committee (AFSC). While they did not achieve, in the long run, all they hoped to, the AFSC went with all their previous positive work as a demonstration of "being for." Even the Nazis knew of their work after WWI feeding starving people in the devasted post-war Germany. Perhaps, though we likely will never know, some of those who became Nazis had been fed by the AFSC.

What we do know is that by being for, the AFSC, along with the Friends Service Council in Britain, won the Nobel Peace Prize in 1947. As the Nobel's website notes, the AFSC had assisted in the rebuilding of France after WWI, provided livestock and seed corn, organized impressive aid projects in Germany and the Soviet Union, worked on behalf of Jewish refugees, and cared for victims on both sides in the Spanish Civil War.

The Nobel committee praised the Friends Service Council for continuing British Quakers' long tradition based on "the belief that God's goodness shows itself in good deeds" and noted that the prize "marked the Nobel Committee's recognition both of pioneering work in the international peace movement and of humanitarian work carried out without regard for race or nationality."[5]

Now Jones, Yarnell, and Walton went to Germany on behalf of an organization, as have other Quakers through the years. But that doesn't mean only organizations can be for – individuals can, and need to be, as well.

When I think of people who are for something instead of against, my friend Shelley Newby comes to mind. Shelley and I were members of a Quaker meeting in New Castle, Indiana awhile back. In April of 2005 she had a vision of herself walking a long distance. Over time the vision became a faith journey which lead her to walk for peace from our small city in eastern Indiana to Washington, DC, a journey of over 500 miles. She meant for each step to be a prayer for peace.

Now when Shelley got this vision, she was no spry athletic 20-year-old. She was a mother of three nearing age 50.

Shelly didn't start walking the day her vision came to her. In good Quaker fashion she spent time seasoning her leading. Testing it. Which meant, in part, spending a lot of time in conditioning and planning. These are things she says are not part of her nature. As the time approached for her to begin her trek, she was walking 90 miles a week and had plans for where she would spend most nights.

Shelley said that her hopes for her peace pilgrimage were:

- that when people saw a nearly 50-year-old, nonathletic woman walking for peace, they might be stirred to ask themselves what they might do.
- that she might stimulate prayer and hope for peace and faith; that it is even possible through faith.
- that she might be inspired by the people she met and their hopes and visions, and then that she might share these hopes and vision with others – including those in the US

government.

- that she could be a part of making known a Christian voice other than the ones that we are hearing so much from lately.
- and that her personal faith and reliance on God would be deepened and expanded.

While walking, Shelley maintained her "for" peace attitude. When others, no matter how well-meaning or sincere, wanted to join with anti-war signs, she asked them not to participate in the walk unless they laid down those signs.

Now did Shelley bring about world peace while walking? No. But she opened conversations with people who might not otherwise have chatted with her had she been an anti-war protestor instead of peace activist.

Another example of keeping it positive is a non-Quaker one I learned of the year I began working on this book. It's the Tiny Pricks Project. This art project was begun by Diana Weymar and invites people from around the world to stitch Donald Trump's words (many of them are from his tweets) onto textiles. She calls it a material record of Donald Trump's presidency, making something permanent (well, as permanent as art can be) in relation to the impermanence of social media and what the participants feel are hurtful, harmful, and hateful statements by the president.

This art movement takes anger, or even rage, and refocuses it into the positive of creating art. And the project has a few guidelines which fit the theme of this chapter:

- Be kind, use kind words even when commenting on the unkind.
- Use art and craft for good – to process and be present.
- Consider culture – how to be civilized, treat each other well.

- Be aware. Find context for quotes and engage even when it's very hard.[6]

In following these guides, the participants have created compelling pieces of art that are fierce in the defense of their values. And some are amazingly beautiful.

Now, throughout Quaker history there have been Friends who didn't model what I've been saying. George Fox and many of the early Friends were often "in your face" individuals, especially when it came to calling out Puritan and other priests and professors. Notice that those they called out were other people of faith. They were less bellicose when it came to addressing those in governmental power. Similar to how Jesus was – confronting the faithful and inviting the "other" to participate in a new way. Benjamin Lay's approach to ending slavery in the Religious Society of Friends certainly didn't avoid vilifying those he opposed. He called the Quaker slaveholders "apostates" – and worse. Even then, I can't help but remember he was talking to the faithful – or those who claimed to be.

The dilemma for many of us is how to be prophetic while still remaining pastoral. How do we speak out forcefully in love? Can it be done? As my friend John Lampen said to me:

There's a place for Benjamin Lay in the antislavery struggle as well as for John Woolman. Some Friends are called to be prophets – to speak out against injustice and evil; there is also a calling to be reconcilers – to bridge differences and heal wounds. But for most of us working in social and international conflicts, it's not possible to do both; it leads to misunderstandings and anger if we try. Each of us must discern which is to be our own specific role and leave other types of action to other people.

There may be people who can disparage those they oppose and still hold to their spiritual anchor. I know, however, I cannot. The moment I begin name-calling – even out of righteous indignation – the spiritual ground shifts under me. The anchor loses its grip. And I'm in danger of doing harm to my own soul.

This isn't about playing it safe – only playing it soul safe. Indeed, being for something can put us in harm's way. Certainly, the three wise men were not in a safe place. Like Daniel who was for his faith in God, they found themselves literally in a lion's den. They came out alive, but there is no guarantee that will always be the case. American Quaker Tom Fox was tortured and then martyred in 2006 when serving with Christian Peacemaker Teams (CPT) in Iraq. CPT is an international organization set up to support teams of peace workers in conflict areas around the world. These teams work for peace through nonviolent direct action and by training local people in nonviolence. CPT sums their work up as "committed to reducing violence by *getting in the way.*"[7] As Tom Fox blogged from Iraq, "If Jesus and Gandhi are right... I am to stand firm against the kidnapper as I am against the soldier. Does that mean I walk into a raging battle to confront the soldiers? Does that mean I walk the streets of Baghdad with a sign saying 'American for the Taking'? No to both counts. But if Jesus and Gandhi are right, then I am asked to risk my life and if I lose it to be as forgiving as they were when murdered by the forces of Satan."[8]

CPT's work shows that being for (in their case being for peace and non-violence) doesn't mean we don't take a stand. Rather, it's about how we make that stand.

Some American Friends have had leadings to go to the southwest border of the United States and provide aid to those who have been victimized by policies of the US government. Some Quakers have been willingly arrested doing non-violent civil disobedience as they stand for basic human rights for immigrants – whether or not the government has declared them legal or illegal.

Being for can mean being for civil disobedience. But it's a civil disobedience that has a certain touch of civility to it. If we are truly non-violent and looking for that of God in all people, then we will not resist arrest or vilify the arresting officers. We may go to jail for justice, but we need to model godliness in our behavior toward others.

Again, this is not easy.

But it is our call.

If, that is, we genuinely want to be the friends of Jesus. And perhaps change those working for empire's hearts and minds. And souls.

Chapter Five

What Is Ours to Do?

There are so many needs and so many wrongs that need righting in our world. Hunger and famine. Racism and white privilege. Economic inequity. Climate change. The list could fill a book. Or two. A question that is often on my mind is "What's mine to do?"

I too easily find myself overwhelmed by that question.

One reason is that I do want to do most everything. Each of these many good things that need doing speaks to a certain part of me, saying, "Do something!" I care about many of these things. I contribute to hunger relief organizations. I've educated myself about and changed my personal behavior around bias issues that I hadn't paid much attention to since my white privilege shielded me from many of their most egregious consequences. I changed the land I live on from production agriculture to native hardwood forest and tall grass prairie to restore wildlife habitat and hopefully improve ground water and air quality.

Those are good things. But they're just a drop in the doing good bucket. A new need greets me almost every day. Or hour. And I want to go to work on it. That's partly because I'm a problem solver – a fixer. I see something amiss and want to fix it, whether it's a dripping faucet, a broken heart, or abuses in the immigration and border control systems. This is not a bad thing – it's just that I need to remember to ask, "What's mine to do?" before just rushing and doing something that may not be the right thing – for the need or for me. Taking time to center myself in the Spirit not only gives me direction regarding what is mine to do, but often opens a fresh new way of doing it. A way that is deeper and more authentic than my instantaneous intellectual solution to the problem. The fresh new way may be, and often is, something that had not occurred to me in my rushing – and I find myself surprised by it in a soul-satisfying way.

John Lampen writes:

> When I am aware of something calling for my attention, and I don't see clearly at first what it is, my response is to wait in the Light. As I make myself still the issue becomes clearer. It may be something wrong in myself, or an outside problem which concerns me. That is followed by a strong sense of the need for action. It may be followed by a conviction of something which I myself should do. The action is often only a first step, and it's usually unclear what the outcome will be. In 1998, I felt a strong call to return to Uganda, ten years after my previous two visits. I could not have said why. And I certainly could not have foreseen the work in landmine issues, peacebuilding, community development, nursery education and adult literacy which flowed from obeying it.[1]

I know I can too easily jump into something, spend energy doing what I consider "the fix" and then move onto the next emerging issue – with the result that nothing much I've done is well done or helpful because it wasn't mine to do. The Quaker practice of waiting in the Light helps me determine what is mine to do… and how, maybe, to do it.

Another reason that question is on my mind is that, because I'm a somewhat public Quaker due to my writing, leading retreats, and the like, many Friends who are involved in various issues push me to be more involved in their cause. They feel I should use my "platform" to call attention to the things they're working on. Those are good things. While I don't want to disappoint my friends, I have to step back and remember that while that particular cause may be their cause, it isn't necessarily mine.

Still, I feel guilty –as if I've been judged by them and found lacking in zeal or dedication to social justice. When I feel that way, I return to the following words by some Friends in the mid-twentieth-century:

> Incomparably the most important thing is that each one of us should be sensitive to the call of God to ourselves and not spend time in passing judgment on the lives of others.... Our duty is to be sensitive to what God is asking us to do, and not to dissipate our energies trying to be absolutists in several directions at once.[2]

Those words remind me that the question is not, "What is good, worthy, important?" but rather "What am I called to do?" This question doesn't just apply to individuals – it's for our faith communities as well.

As we think about that question, we have to realize that we can't do everything. We do not, as individuals or local congregations have the emotional, physical, or spiritual resources to do everything that needs doing. If we try, we run out of spiritual steam. Or get caught up in the paralysis of analysis – looking at things from so many angles and asking questions and raising concerns that we never get anything done.

We also need to realize that while we can't do everything, we can support many things. By that, I mean we can back the efforts of others (individuals and congregations) who are doing the worthy work that isn't our worthy work. For example, my small meeting is genuinely concerned about reaching out to students at a local elementary school that exists in food (and economic) desert. It's just one school. That's what we can take on. We've helped with a tiny space for a clothing closet that a local Girl Scout set up as a service project. But we can't feed the entire township. So we support, monetarily, the groups that are helping to do that, while some people in our Quaker meeting give of our physical energies to the local school children.

We decided what was ours to do via a series of spiritual conversations. Together we talked about ourselves as a meeting, our relative privilege in this place, and our interests. As we did that, some longtime members reminded us that our original meetinghouse was across the street from where the elementary school is located. As we looked around the room, we saw that we had a good number of farmers and schoolteachers in our meeting. As we talked and prayed about the Quaker question "What is ours to do?" it became clear that working with the school was one of those things. Not because it was good or worthy or needed – though it was all those things. Not because it was what we should do. But because if felt like what we were called to do.

We arrived at that decision after a number of tests.

- First, we asked where is this desire to work with local school coming from? We especially wanted to rule out the idea that it might be coming from our egos – "we privileged people can help those poor dears." As we prayed and talked, it became apparent it really came from a love of our community and the desire to work alongside the teachers, administrators, and parents.
- Next, we examined if our task was clear. Did we know what we thought we could do... and not do? It quickly became clear we couldn't do everything we'd like to do, but we could do some things – specific activities that the school people said was needed, such as listening to children read to us as a way of improving their reading and comprehension and (since we have some good cooks in the meeting) providing food for the teachers on parent/teacher conference days.
- Then we looked at whether this work was compelling. We agreed it was and that we could commit to this work because it spoke to our minds, hearts, and souls.

- Next, we checked how it fit with our life and faith as a congregation. When we did that, we remembered that throughout our meeting's history, our members have worked in various educational settings in places of need – from East Africa in the '50s and '60s to Belize in the twenty-first century. Now we had the opportunity to work just down the street.

- We kept asking, does our desire to do this come from God's love? We decided that we couldn't teach our own children to sing "Jesus loves the little children" if that love didn't motivate us to help the children one half mile away. Quaker Jennifer Kavanagh says, "Love finds expression in action."[3] Likewise, our action has to be an expression, an outgrowth, of love.

- We also considered the thought that doing what God wants us to do always changes people and congregations. So, we asked how it would change us. One of the ways is that we would no longer have our (mostly unused) coat room and library overflow to ourselves. A minor change, but a change. Another way was that we would have to give up our time to drive (most of us do not live in the vicinity of the meeting) to the school to do our volunteer work.

Now this is a small work. But then we're a small meeting. But we resonate with Deborah Haines who said:

> I think I have wasted a great deal of my life waiting to be called to some great mission which would change the world. I have looked for important social movements. I have wanted to make a big and important contribution to the causes I believe in. I think I have been too ready to reject the genuine leadings I have been given as being matters of little consequence. It has taken me a long time to learn that obedience means doing what we are called to do even if it seems pointless or

unimportant or even silly. The great social movements of our time may well be part of our calling. The ideals of peace and justice and equality which are part of our religious tradition are often the focus of debate. But we cannot simply immerse ourselves in these activities. We need to develop our own unique social witness, in obedience to God. We need to listen to the gentle whispers which will tell us how we can bring our lives into greater harmony with heaven.[4]

And, indeed, that this was our work to do was confirmed in a lovely way when the principal of the school came to meeting for worship one Sunday, sat with us, and then thanked us for our efforts.

Now that's not to say we've always gotten things right. A few years back, because of hunger in our area, we thought we'd do a neighborhood garden. After a quick discussion we decided to plow up part of our side yard, put in a garden, and offer plots to people in the area. One fellow (me) had seen such plots while riding the train to the Quaker office in Philadelphia and thought it was a grand idea. It was a grand idea, but not something people wanted, evidently. To paraphrase an old movie line, we built it, but they did not come.

That re-taught us that decisions/leadings need to be seasoned as Quakers say. In the same way throwing some spices into meal prep at the last minutes does not result in the same savory result as giving them time to imbue the meal with all their zesty flavor. Decisions need to be seasoned as well. So we try to do that.

Now before you think that our work with the school is the only work we do, it's not. It's just one example. It is one that takes a lot of energy. But as a community of faith we also pass minutes (Quakerese for formal statements) about issues and send to local papers and other media and our local, state, government officials. Two recent ones have been about banning the sale of assault style weapons and high capacity magazines and in favor of our state adopting anti-bias/hate crimes legislation. Those are issues that have long been close to our members' hearts. We've also made contributions to groups providing direct assistance to immigrants on the United States' southern border since we, located 1500 miles away, can't do it in person.

We also realize that we, as a meeting, do not have to do everything together. Individual members work at domestic violence shelters, community centers, and as political lobbyists. All in the name of the gospel as we understand it. The collective we can't do everything, but we can support most everything.

Throughout the years, Quakers have discovered some signs of work that is ours. These include sensations of:

- Love – does the work warm our hearts and souls? Does it pump energy into us?
- Caring – does it tender our hearts? Or do we feel like we must grit our teeth and do it because of obligation?
- Beauty – will we be creating something beautiful? Turning something ugly into something pleasing?
- Persistence – does it keep coming to us? Or is it something like a good idea but one that soon passes? If it hangs around, that's a good sign that it's ours to do.
- Rightness – is it aligned with who we are, what we believe, our desires, and our abilities? Does it fit with our lives as individuals or a congregation?
- Feeling in harmony with God – how does it fit with what we know (no matter how little we know) of the Divine?

Another thing Quakers have learned is that while action should follow a time of discerning and seasoning, that doesn't mean that discernment is over. In fact, it is continuous and ongoing – like a spiritual mobius strip. We sense work that is ours to do. We wait and test that (the time length of testing and waiting vary on the urgency and the amount of time it takes to reach clarity).

We act. We continue sensing whether this work is still ours to do. We wait for clarity. We act.

There may be a time during the sensing and waiting that we discern that the work we've been doing is no longer ours to do. That it is time to lay it down (Quakerese for stop doing it) or hand it off to others. If that's the case, then we should view that as a Divine opportunity to do something new.

As we individually and collectively consider what is ours to do, we have to realize that we might feel judged by others whose work is different than ours. Or, even worse, we might judge others whose work is different than ours. That's why it's wise to remember the Friends' words I quoted earlier – "Incomparably the most important thing is that each one of us should be sensitive to the call of God to ourselves and not spend time in passing judgment on the lives of others."[5] As Margaret Glover wrote:

> Those of us known as 'activists' have sometimes been hurt by the written or spoken implication that we must be spending too little time on our spiritual contemplative lives. [F]or those of us who are Friends, our attendance at meeting for worship and our silent prayerful times are what make our outer activity viable and effective – if it is effective.[6]

Her words remind us that Quaker hope, witness, and action are grounded in the life of the Spirit. Or at least they need to be if we want them to be effective and sustainable. Being grounded in a deep life of our soul helps us tap into resources beyond ourselves. It sustains us when we grow weary or fear that our work and witness is in vain. This grounding means, as Glover points out, that we need a communal spiritual life as well as a personal one. We benefit from being part of a faith community that loves us, supports us, guides us, and even corrects us if we run too far ahead of our spiritual Guide.

Glover also wrote:

I have similarly seen quieter Friends hurt by the implication that they do not care enough, because they are not seen to be "politically active". Some worry unnecessarily that they may be doing things of a "less important" nature, as if to be seen doing things by the eyes of the world is the same thing as to be seen doing things by the eyes of God.[7]

There is work enough for all of us who endeavor to be people of faith and goodwill. For some it will be the work of prayer and letter writing. For others it will be direct action on the front lines, placing ourselves in harm's way or dishing meals at a local shelter. For some it will be an engagement with the arts – painting, writing poems, performing music, scripting a play – when they come out of a Quaker stillness, these are also contributions which may be our personal calling toward hope and witness. Quaker singer/songwriter Carrie Newcomer is a good example of this. In addition to writing hopeful and encouraging lyrics for dangerous times such as:

The shadows of this world will say,
There's no hope why try anyway?
But every kindness large or slight,
Shifts the balance toward the light.[8]

She works with fellow Friend Parker J. Palmer on the Growing Edge Project.[9] It uses online conversations, spoken words and music, and more in engaging participants in looking at the growing edges of their lives personally, vocationally, and politically.

Likewise, some will plant trees or community gardens. For others it will be a combination of the above things. Or some other surprising things. Regardless, we must test "What is mine (ours) to do?" And then do it.

When we do what is ours to do, we will be more than faithful. We will be effective in amazing ways.

Chapter Six

What Will It Look Like?

Amnesty International. Doctors Without Borders (Médecins Sans Frontières). The World Wildlife Fund. Oxfam. Anti-Vivisection Coalition. The world is filled with worthy organizations doing important and much needed work. People, including Quakers, around the globe are working with these groups on issues like peace, climate change, immigration concerns, food and nutrition, education, medical relief, and so much more. Indeed Quakers were the principal founders of Amnesty International and Oxfam.

So how does a Quaker-specific hope and witness differ from them? How does it look any different? Why not just chuck it in and go to work for one of these fine organizations?

To answer the second question first, to the outward observer, at first glance, it may not look any different. In that way it's similar to a casual observer peering into a meetinghouse window and seeing a group of people sitting in silence. To them it may look like a Buddhist assembly or meditation class. It is only after Quaker worship is fully experienced that one comprehends the difference. The same is true of secular organizations' work and Quaker action. Outwardly they may be doing many of the same activities. However, there's a distinctly different spiritual flavor to the two. More about that later.

Now for the third question – why not just go work with one of these other organizations. In fact, many Quakers do. I, included. As I mentioned earlier, I have a special interest in conservation efforts. That's one reason the land where I live has had 20,000 trees planted and countless wildflower and warm season grass seeds spread in the last fifteen years. Because of my environmental concerns I support both the National Wildlife

Federation and Quaker Earthcare Witness (QEW). Each align with my concern for care of the earth. QEW, though, also speaks to my doing what I do from a spiritual point of view. It provides me with resources that enhance my spirit while I do this work.

And now for the first question. How does Quaker hope and witness differ from the work others are doing? That's in the flavor that I mentioned earlier.

As I said, Quakers often talk about seasoning a leading or a possible action before getting to work. In the same way the right amount spices and seasonings lead to a tasty repast, so do Quaker principles season our hope and witness. Now it is true that a meal without spices may be wholesome and nutritious, but a meal correctly seasoned satisfies us in ways that are more than just giving us fuel for daily living. Quaker spices flavor our work and witness in ways that give it a unique flavor compared to the excellent work done by our justice co-workers. The spices we add are known as the testimonies – what we have to say about important facets of our faith. They are not some quirky Quaker add-on, but rather what we understand about how we are to live out the gospel of Christ in our daily lives. They are spicy. Perhaps that's why the acronym SPICES has been used as a sort of spiritual shorthand to say what our Quaker testimonies in this time are:

S – simplicity
P – peace
I – integrity
C – community
E – equality
S – stewardship of the earth.

Those testimonies are ingredients that add savor and flavor to our witness, indeed. A dash of simplicity, a pinch of peace, et al., are needed to keep our work grounded in our principles. They hopefully also keep us from just being a bunch of well-meaning do-gooders who could do more harm than good.

So how do these things inform our witness and action? Regardless of what we are called to do – work for peace, care of the earth, immigration reform, and so on – they each need to be present in some degree for our Quaker work to be fully in line with our faith.

We need **simplicity** in all we do because it encompasses so much more than the common understanding of it as living in a one-room cabin à la Henry David Thoreau or eschewing consumerism. It is, as Lloyd Lee Wilson says, "the name we give to our effort to free ourselves to give full attention to God's still, small voice: the sum of our efforts to subtract from our lives everything that competes with God for our attention and clear hearing."[1]

Simplicity helps us strip away all that is not needed to do our work and witness. Organizations often talk about mission creep – taking on good projects that don't fully align with their purpose. The end result is that their good work gets diluted or fractured. Simplicity keeps our focus on what we're called to do.

Peace, likewise, informs our work and witness. It would be terribly silly for Quakers to work for peace if the work itself was fraught with dissension. Or if what we do results in actually bringing about armed conflict.

I'm not talking here about avoiding civil disobedience – which could lead to violence on the part of some. I am saying that our witness, when it is rooted in Quaker principles, will always be non-violent on our part. Both physically and emotionally. That's what the Quaker Bayard Rustin taught Martin Luther King, Jr. While we all learned as children the saying "Sticks and stones may break my bones, but words will never hurt me," we know that just isn't true. Words do wound. They scar. And so, as we take a stand for peace or immigration reform or get ourselves arrested, we need to do so in a spirit of peace. We must be peaceful in our souls and in our actions toward those who are handcuffing us. Our words must be of blessing. Not curse.

Our work and witness need to have **integrity** – both with who we are as individuals of faith and also our community of faith. They must be true to what we say we believe and how we live. If we say we're a peaceful people, for example, but lack inner peace, then a lack of integrity will be obvious in our peace work. Likewise, our saying we have witness for inclusion for all people can't be shown to be a lie by our excluding anyone. This may be easy to do in cases of race or gender issues. What about if it excludes those from a different political party or social class?

The testimony of **community** instructs us how we are to live and work together. What are the ingredients of community? For Quakers, first and foremost, it is rooted in a spiritually gathered people. We try, when we are at our best, in our meetings to be places where each voice is heard and where we seek the mind and heart of the Divine together. That's why we make decisions as a community, not by majority rule or Roberts Rules of Order. For us, true community says, when a decision is reached, "This is what we believe God's direction for us is." This testimony of community informs our witness and work in this world – including us all in the work and the decisions related to that work.

Equality reminds us that we are in this together. Not just all us Quakers but all humanity. The testimony of equality helps us remember that, in daily life as well as worthy work, this is not about the privileged inviting the underprivileged to our well set table, but rather that all people are invited to God's table. The beloved community is not about white people making room for people of color. Rather it is about recognizing that humans cannot create God's beloved community until everyone has an equal place in that community.

Stewardship of the earth must be a part of all we do, as well. What does our use of earth-based resources say about our work and witness? From paper to fossil fuels to the food we eat and more. If our activity, no matter how worthy, harms the planet, is it rightly ordered, as Quakers say? Audrey Urry said:

> All species and the Earth itself have interdependent roles within Creation.... All parts, all issues, are inextricably intertwined. Indeed the web of creation could be described as of three-ply thread: wherever we touch it we affect justice and peace and the health of all everywhere. So all our testimonies, all our Quaker work, all our Quaker lives are part of one process, of striving towards a flourishing, just and peaceful Creation—the Kingdom of God.[2]

By seasoning our work with these SPICES, we create, in the words of Dominican priest and theologian Gustavo Gutiérrez:

> [A] theology which does not stop with reflecting on the world, but rather tries to be a process through which the world is transformed. It is a theology which is open – in the protest against trampled human dignity, in the struggle against the plunder of the vast majority of people, in liberating love, and in the building of a new, just, and fraternal society – to the gift of the Kingdom of God.[3]

The SPICES are a Quaker gift to the kingdom – and kin-dom (people) – of God. So, what does it look like to have work seasoned with simplicity, integrity, community, equality, and earth stewardship?

One example is Quaker Voluntary Service (QVS). I'm on the board of directors for QVS so am not completely impartial, but I've found that this organization provides an opportunity for young adults in sympathy with Quaker principles to spend almost a year living "at the intersection of transformational spirituality and activism" incorporates the SPICES into its work.

The fellows, as they are called, work full-time in community organizations (mostly non-Quaker ones) that advocate for racial justice, economic justice, environmental sustainability, women's rights, and more. As part of the experience they live in a cooperative house. They worship with and are mentored by local Quakers. The young adults receive housing, transportation, food, support for health and wellness, and a small stipend. They engage in regular self-led workshops and retreats that allow for continuing education in social justice, faith, and community building topics. All of these, including their work, worship, compensation, and living arrangements, are consistent with the testimonies of simplicity, peace, integrity, community, equality, earth stewardship. As is the board's decision-making process.

QVS has more than 200 alumni. Many of these young adults are still at work with organizations they spent their fellowship with or in a similar field. And they report that they are putting the essential Quaker principles they learned to work in their vocations and daily lives. There are programs similar to QVS in the United Kingdom and at the Quaker United Nations Offices in Geneva and New York.

Another group putting the SPICES into its work is Friends Peace Teams (FPT). FPT members are spread around the globe. They have wide-ranging work, including with those who are incarcerated, prison guard and law enforcement, refugees, survivors of violence and war, victims of human trafficking and more. One of their projects is Healing and Rebuilding Our Communities (HROC). HROC was developed in the Great Lakes region of east Africa to engage participants in looking at and talking about the consequences of violence in their lives. It does so in part by bringing people from opposing sides of a conflict together in this work – a true example of the Quaker principle of looking for that of God in the other. Even if the other is an enemy.

These are just two examples of organizations based on the

Quaker testimonies and how the testimonies come into play both in the work and witness. There are many others (you'll find a partial list in the appendix). And they each show the spiritual power of hope and witness based in the Quaker testimonies. These are testimonies that any person or organization of faith can use in their own setting.

They are the spices of the spiritual life.

Chapter Seven

So, Where's the Hope?

I was talking with my late good friend and Quaker Alan one day about hope. "I have found life is easier," he said, "when you've given up all hope."

I was taken aback by his statement. I'd always thought of him as a person of extreme creativity, vitality and imagination. He was the sort who seemed to bring ideas to life in new and exciting ways. That, to me, embodies the essence of optimism – hope. He worked for racial inclusion, education for all people, and feeding the hungry. He didn't seem the sort who had given up hope.

As I later reflected on what he said, I thought there were two ways I could look at his statement. One way was as an expression of despair – "abandon all hope ye who enter here." The other way to see it is as a positive truth.

Let's look at the despair part first. There are times when life seems hopeless. After all, as one wag put it, none of us get out of here alive. Hope. It often seems difficult to hold onto in dangerous times. We can easily be overwhelmed by the massive amounts of injustice and suffering in the world and the amount of work that has to be done. There may be times we feel like throwing our hands up in surrender. Yet, hope is vital. And hope is not misplaced if placed in that which is Eternal.

Which brings me to seeing Alan's statement as something positive. He, like many other Friends, put his hope in that which lasts. In that, he had learned the truth of George Fox's words to Quakers in the midst of harsh persecution in 1663:

Sing and rejoice, ye Children of the Day and of the Light; for the Lord is at work in this thick night of Darkness that may be felt: and Truth doth flourish as the rose, and the lilies do grow among the thorns, and the plants atop of the hills, and upon them the lambs doth skip and play. And never heed the tempests nor the storms, floods nor rains, for the Seed Christ is over all and doth reign. And so, be of good faith and valiant for the Truth.[1]

In the "thick night of Darkness" the "Truth doth flourish as a rose." Fox was reminding his readers, and us today, that God's truth will triumph. We do well to hold to that hope. The apostle Paul wrote, "whatever we may have to go through is no less than nothing compared with the magnificent future God has planned for us. The whole creation waits on tiptoe to see the wonderful sight of the children of God coming into their own."[2]

And therein lies the positive truth of Alan's statement. If we have given up hope in our intellect, emotions, and limited perception of reality, then we have cleared the way for the true hope. This hope, according to Paul, is that "in the end the whole of created life will be rescued from the tyranny of change and decay, and have its share in the magnificent liberty which can only belong to the children of God."[3]

As children of God, friends of Jesus, we are invited to work with God in the redemption of the world in ways that feed our souls while caring for others. A work and witness rooted in the life of spirit is one of hope. It leads us from hateful words and actions to healing words and actions. It is a life of radical hope that stands in stark contrast to the attitudes and actions of people who would harm and divide us all.

Eberhard Arnold, the founder of the Bruderhof, though not a Quaker had much in sympathy with Friends. He wrote:

Our expectation of the kingdom cannot be a passive waiting, a sweet, soft occupation with ourselves and our like-minded friends. No, if we truly expect God's kingdom, we will be filled with divine power. Then the social justice of the future – with its purity of heart and divine fellowship – will be realized now, wherever Jesus himself is present. Our belief in the future must bring change to the present! The spirit of expectation is the spirit of action because it is the spirit of faith. Faith is bravery. Faith is reality. If we have faith, even only a small seed, we cannot regard anything as impossible.[4]

Nothing is impossible. As my friend Carrie Newcomer sings:

It's impossible, impossible.
Impossible, until it's not.[5]

With spiritual grounding and trust in that which is eternal, hope is not a silly, foolish notion. Rather it is a realistic, eyes wide-open view to the facts of injustice and want in this world sort of hope that calls us to healing, courageous, and compassionate work and witness. It's a hope that helps us remember those who worked for these same things in generations past. With Divine assistance, they brought about many improvements in people's lives and society at large. So shall we.

We are not alone but surrounded by the Spirit of God and our past co-workers' witness and empowered by their vision and hope. We may not achieve all our goals. Realistically, we know we won't. But still, with Divine assistance, we can together make a very real difference in our hurting, suffering world.

In doing so, we will, as first Friend George Fox said, "Be patterns, be examples in all countries, places, islands, nations, wherever you come, that your carriage and life may preach among all sorts of people, and to them; then you will come to walk cheerfully over the world, answering that of God in everyone."[4]

A cheerful, expectant, life-changing – for us and those we

work for and with – hope awaits us. It beckons us forward. Forward. Forward. To a faith that matters now.

Appendix: Quaker Organizations at Work in the World

There are a plethora of Quaker groups implanting Friends principles and doing hopeful witness work in the world. Below is a sampling of these hard-working organizations.

Advocacy

Friends Committee on National Legislation –
https://www.fcnl.org/
Quaker Asylum and Refugee Network, UK –
http://www.qarn.org.uk/
Quaker Council for European Affairs –
http://www.qcea.org/
Quaker United Nations Office –
https://quno.org/

Change

Alternatives to Violence Project Britain
https://avpbritain.org/
Alternatives to Violence Project USA
https://avpusa.org/
Children's Creative Response to Conflict –
http://crc-global.org/
Progresa (Guatemala Friends Scholarship Program)
www.guatemalafriends.org
Toward Right Relationship with Native People –
https://friendspeaceteams.org/trr/
Turning the Tide (nonviolent social development) –
https://turningtide.org.uk/
West Midlands Quaker Peace Education Programme –
http://peacemakers.org.uk

Development

Friendly Water for the World –
https://friendlywater.org/
Quaker Bolivia Link –
https://qbl.org/
Quaker Service Australia –
https://qsa.org.au/
Quaker Service (Northern Ireland) –
www.quakerservice.com/
Money for Madagascar –
https://moneyformadagascar.org/

Environmental and Ecojustice

Earth Quaker Action Team –
https://www.eqat.org/
Quaker Earthcare Witness –
https://www.quakerearthcare.org/
Quakers in Britain – Sustainability –
https://www.quaker.org.uk/our-work/sustainability

Service and Peace Work

American Friends Service Committee –
https://www.afsc.org/
Canadian Friends Service Committee –
https://quakerservice.ca/
Friends House Moscow –
https://friendshousemoscow.org/
Friends Peace Teams –
https://friendspeaceteams.org/
Quaker House –
https://quakerhouse.org/
Quaker Peace and Social Witness UK –
https://www.quaker.org.uk/our-work

Quaker Social Action –
https://quakersocialaction.org.uk/
Quaker Voluntary Service –
https://www.quakervoluntaryservice.org/
Youth Service Opportunities Project –
http://www.ysop.org/

Chapter Notes

Introduction

1   James 2:17.

2   Robert Short, *The Gospel According to Peanuts* (New York: Bantam Books, 1968), p. 5.

3   Matthew 25:35–40.

4   John 15:14–15.

5   William Penn, *No Cross, No Crown, Seventh Edition* (London: John Sowle, 1725), p. 77.

6   https://www.rustincenter.org/

Chapter One

1   Daniel 2:44.

2   Rudolf W. Heinze, *Reform and Conflict: From the Medieval World to the Wars of Religion AD 1350–1658* (Oxford: Monarch Books, 2005), p. 464.

3   George Fox, *The Journal of George Fox: A Revised Edition by John L. Nickalls* (London: Religious Society of Friends, 1975), p. 11.

4   John 1:9.

5   Geoffrey Durham, *What Do Quakers Believe* (Alresford, Hampshire: John Hunt Publishing, 2019), p. 28.

6   Stephen B. Baxter, *Basic Documents of English History* (Boston: Houghton Mifflin, 1968), pp 139, 142.

7   George Fox, *The Journal of George Fox: A Revised Edition by John L. Nickalls* (London: Religious Society of Friends, 1975), p. 398.

8   Tim Gee, *Why I am a Pacifist: A Call for a More Nonviolent World* (Alresford, Hampshire: John Hunt Publishing, 2019), p. 36.

Chapter Two

1 Paula Palmer, Quaker Indian Boarding Schools, Friends Journal, https://www.friendsjournal.org/quaker-indian-boarding-schools/

2 ibid.

3 Eva I. Pinthus, "Faith and Politics Hand in Hand," *The Friend, Vol 145* (1987), p. 483.

4 Harvey Gillman, *A Light That Is Shining: An Introduction to the Quakers* (London: Quaker Home Service, 1988), pp 48–49.

5 Eva I. Pinthus, "Faith and Politics Hand in Hand," *The Friend, Vol 145* (1987), p. 483.

6 https://www.afsc.org/sites/default/files/documents/Our_Day_in_the_German_Gestapo_by_Rufus_Jones.pdf

7 Rhiannon Grant, *Telling the Truth about God: Quaker Approaches to Theology* (Barnett (Alresford, Hampshire: John Hunt Publishing, 2019), p.21.

8 Craig Barnett, *The Guided Life: Finding Purpose in Troubled Times* (Alresford, Hampshire: John Hunt Publishing, 2019), p. 31.

9 ibid.

10 Lucy Fryer Morland, *The New Social Outlook* (London: The Woodbrooke Extension Committee, 1918) p.45.

11 John Woolman, *The Journal and Major Essays of John Woolman*, Phillips P. Moulton, editor (New York: Oxford University Press, 1971) p. 122.

12 ibid, p. 127.

13 Roger Wilson, "Silver and Gold Have I None," *Public Resources and Private Lives: Some Quaker Views on Equity and Our Economic Problems*, Jim Platts and David Eversly, editors (London: Social Responsibility Council of the Religious Society of Friends, 1976) pp. 225–226.

Chapter 3

1 Martin Luther King, Jr., *The Papers of Martin Luther King, Jr.*,

Volume III, Birth of a New Age, December 1955–December 1956, Clayborne Carson, editor (Berkeley: University of California Press, 1997) p. 259.

2   William C. Braithwaite, *The Second Period of Quakerism* (York: William Sessions Limited, 1979) pp. 596–597.

3   Jo Vallacott in *Reweaving the Web of Life: Feminism and Nonviolence,* Pam McAllister, editor (Philadelphia: New Society Publishers, 1982), p. 34.

4   Gordon Matthews, "Mixing Prayer and Politics," *The Friend, Vol 147* (1989), p. 717.

5   William Penn, *Fruits of Solitude in Reflections and Maxims Relating to the Conduct of Life* (Philadelphia: Friends Book Store, n.d.), p 27.

6   Inazo Nitobe, *Selections from Inazo Nitobe's Writings,* Tadeo Yanaihara (Japan: Nitobe Memorial Fund, 1936), p.159.

7   Thomas Merton, *Conjectures of Guilty Bystander* (New York: Image Books, 2009), p. 81.

8   Brother Lawrence quoted in *Essential Mystic Prayers* (Brewster, MA: Paraclete Press, 2018), p. 53.

Chapter Four

1   Oscar Arnulfo Romero, *The Violence of Love* (Walden, NY: Plough Publishing House, 1998) p. 123.

2   https://www.afsc.org/sites/default/files/documents/Our_ Day_in_the_German_Gestapo_by_Rufus_Jones.pdf

3   Luke 5:32.

4   Diana Lampen in *Faith in Action: Encounters with Friends* (London: Friends World Committee for Consultation, 1992), p. 71.

5   https://www.nobelpeaceprize.org/Prize-winners/ Prizewinner-documentation/The-Friends-Service-Council-The-American-Friends-Service-Committee-the-Quakers

6   Diana Weymar and the Tiny Pricks Project https://www. tinypricksproject.com/

7   https://cpt.org/

8   Tom Fox, Fight or Flight, http://waitinginthelight.blogspot. com/2004/10/fight-or-flight.html.

Chapter 5

1   John Lampen, *Quaker Roots and Branches* (Alresford, Hampshire: John Hunt Publishing, 2018), p. 58.

2   Industry and the Social Order Conference, 1958 quoted in *Quaker Faith and Practice, Second Edition* (London: Yearly Meeting of the Religious Society of Friends (Quakers) in Britain, 1995), 20:25.

3   Jennifer Kavanagh, *Practical Mystics: Quaker Faith in Action* (Alresford, Hampshire: John Hunt Publishing, 2019), p. 35.

4   Deborah Haines, "Living in Harmony with Heaven on Earth," *Friends Search for Wholeness*, John L. Bond, editor (Richmond, IN: Friends United Press, 1978), p. 139.

5   Industry and the Social Order Conference, 1958 quoted in *Quaker Faith and Practice, Second Edition* (London: Yearly Meeting of the Religious Society of Friends (Quakers) in Britain, 1995), 20:25.

6   Margaret Glover, Letter to the Editor, *The Friend, Volume 147* (1989), p. 830.

7   ibid.

8   Carrie Newcomer, "Lean in Toward the Light," words and Music by Carrie Newcomer ©2016 Carrie Newcomer Music (BMI), Administered by BMG Chrysalis.

9   https://www.newcomerpalmer.com/

Chapter Six

1   Lloyd Lee Wilson, "Discernment: Coming Under the Guidance of the Holy Spirit," *Journal of the North Carolina Yearly Meeting (Conservative), Number 6* (n. p., 2012), page 2.

2   Audrey Urry quoted in *Quaker Faith and Practice, Second Edition* (London: Yearly Meeting of the Religious Society of

Friends (Quakers) in Britain, 1995), 25.04

2   Gustavo Gutiérrez, A Theology of Liberation: History, Politics, Salvation (Maryknoll: Orbis Books, 1973), p. 13.

Chapter Seven

1   George Fox quoted in quoted in *Quaker Faith and Practice, Second Edition* (London: Yearly Meeting of the Religious Society of Friends (Quakers) in Britain, 1995), 20:23.

2   Romans 8:19

3   Romans 8:21.

3   Eberhard Arnold, *Writings Selected*, (Walden, NY, Plough Publishing House, 2011).

4   Carrie Newcomer, "Impossible Until It's Not," words and Music by Carrie Newcomer ©2019 Carrie Newcomer Music (BMI), Administered by BMG Chrysalis.

4   George Fox, *The Journal of George Fox: A Revised Edition by John L. Nickalls* (London: Religious Society of Friends, 1975), p. 263.

About Brent

J. Brent Bill is a Quaker minister, author, retreat leader, conservationist, and photographer. He has authored many books, articles, and fiction pieces and teaches writing at graduate school level and in adult continuing education courses. Brent holds degrees from Wilmington College and in Quaker Studies from Earlham School of Religion (a Quaker theological school).

He lives on Ploughshares Farm, forty acres of former Indiana farmland that is being restored to tall grass prairie and native Indiana hardwood forest.

In addition to his ministry of writing, Brent also enjoys a ministry of leading workshops and speaking. Some of his most popular workshops are:

- Beauty, Truth, Life, and Love: A Pilgrimage on Positive Spirituality: In this retreat, we explore how to be reawakened to the fact that everyday life can be infused with God-drenched meaning, inspired and motivated to live a more Spirit-centered existence drenched in beauty, truth, life, and love, and be encouraged to see stories of the beauty, truth, life, love in our own stories.
- Life Lessons from A Bad Quaker: A light-hearted, but serious, workshop for anyone who is bad at being good. With whimsy, humor, and wisdom, workshop participants will explore how to live a life that is simple yet satisfying, peaceful yet strong.
- The Sacred Compass: Spiritual Practices for Discernment is a workshop for those who want to learn discernment as a life process.
- Writing from the Heart: Telling Your Soul's Stories is for those who want to unlock their spiritual stories.
- Being Quiet: The Practice of Holy Silence is based on

Quaker silence and teaches how to be quiet and still in our souls amid the clamor of everyday life.

If you would like more information about Brent's writing, his spirituality workshops and retreats, or would like to contact him about other speaking engagements, you can reach him through his website at www.brentbill.com or via e-mail at brentbil@brentbill.com.

THE NEW OPEN SPACES

Throughout the two thousand years of Christian tradition there
have been, and still are, groups and individuals that exist in
the margins and upon the edge of faith. But in Christianity's
contrapuntal history it has often been these outcasts and
pioneers that have forged contemporary orthodoxy out
of former radicalism as belief evolves to engage with and
encompass the ever-changing social and scientific realities. Real
faith lies not in the comfortable certainties of the Orthodox,
but somewhere in a half-glimpsed hinterland on the dirt track
to Emmaus, where the Death of God meets the Resurrection,
where the supernatural Christ meets the historical Jesus,
and where the revolution liberates both the oppressed and
the oppressors.

Welcome to Christian Alternative... a space at the edge where
the light shines through.
If you have enjoyed this book, why not tell other readers by
posting a review on your preferred book site.
Recent bestsellers from Christian Alternative are:

Bread Not Stones
The Autobiography of An Eventful Life
Una Kroll
The spiritual autobiography of a truly remarkable woman
and a history of the struggle for ordination in the Church of
England.
Paperback: 978-1-78279-804-0 ebook: 978-1-78279-805-7

The Quaker Way
A Rediscovery
Rex Ambler
Although fairly well known, Quakerism is not well understood.
The purpose of this book is to explain how Quakerism works as
a spiritual practice.
Paperback: 978-1-78099-657-8 ebook: 978-1-78099-658-5

Blue Sky God
The Evolution of Science and Christianity
Don MacGregor
Quantum consciousness, morphic fields and blue-sky
thinking about God and Jesus the Christ.
Paperback: 978-1-84694-937-1 ebook: 978-1-84694-938-8

Celtic Wheel of the Year
Tess Ward
An original and inspiring selection of prayers combining
Christian and Celtic Pagan traditions, and interweaving their
calendars into a single pattern of prayer for every morning
and night of the year.
Paperback: 978-1-90504-795-6

Christian Atheist
Belonging without Believing
Brian Mountford
Christian Atheists don't believe in God but miss him: especially the transcendent beauty of his music, language, ethics, and community.
Paperback: 978-1-84694-439-0 ebook: 978-1-84694-929-6

Compassion Or Apocalypse?
A Comprehensible Guide to the Thoughts of René Girard
James Warren
How René Girard changes the way we think about God and the Bible, and its relevance for our apocalypse-threatened world.
Paperback: 978-1-78279-073-0 ebook: 978-1-78279-072-3

Diary Of A Gay Priest
The Tightrope Walker
Rev. Dr. Malcolm Johnson
Full of anecdotes and amusing stories, but the Church is still a dangerous place for a gay priest.
Paperback: 978-1-78279-002-0 ebook: 978-1-78099-999-9

Do You Need God?
Exploring Different Paths to Spirituality Even For Atheists
Rory J.Q. Barnes
An unbiased guide to the building blocks of spiritual belief.
Paperback: 978-1-78279-380-9 ebook: 978-1-78279-379-3

Readers of ebooks can buy or view any of these bestsellers by clicking on the live link in the title. Most titles are published in paperback and as an ebook. Paperbacks are available in traditional bookshops. Both print and ebook formats are available online.

Find more titles and sign up to our readers' newsletter at
http://www.johnhuntpublishing.com/christianity
Follow us on Facebook at
https://www.facebook.com/ChristianAlternative